Restoring the heart & influence of
women in marriage, church,
leadership, sexuality, and life...
without sabotaging the dignity of men.

BRUCE LENGEMAN

Copyright © 2022 by Bruce Lengeman

All rights reserved. This book is protected by the copyright laws of the United States of America. This book may not be copied or reprinted for commercial gain or profit. The use of short quotations or occasional page copying for personal or group study is permitted and encouraged. Permission will be granted upon request.

Scripture quotations, unless otherwise indicated, are taken from the *Holy Bible, New International Version*®. NIV®. Copyright © 1973, 1978, 1984 by International Bible Society. Used by permission of Zondervan. All rights reserved.

Additional Scripture quotations marked KJV are from the Holy Bible, from the *Holy Bible, King James Version*. KJV. Public Domain.

FIRST EDITION

ISBN: 978-1-953576-20-0

Library of Congress Control Number: 2021925639

Published by

3741 Linden Avenue SE | Grand Rapids, MI 49548

Printed in the United States

Disclaimer: The views and opinions expressed in this book are solely those of the author and other contributors. These views and opinions do not necessarily represent those of Certa Publishing. Please note that Certa Publishing's publishing style capitalizes certain pronouns in Scripture that refer to the Father, Son, and Holy Spirit, and may differ from some publishers' styles.

Voice:

One's opinion, view, comment, feeling, wish, desire, vote, knowledge, idea, sensing, caution, influence

"There is neither Jew nor Greek, there is neither slave nor free, there is neither male nor female; for you are all one in Christ Jesus." (Galatians 3:28)

"Good stuff that needs shouted from the mountain top!"

—*Pre-publishing reviewer*

Table of Contents

1	A Lesser Species?	7
2	7 Essential Points That Will Help You Understand the Focus of *Voice!*	11
3	Screwed-Up Theology and the Glory of an Ezer	17
4	The "Lesser Woman" Concept Revealed at a Couples' Meeting	21
5	Whatever Happened to Verse 21?	25
6	I Know It's True When We Go Out to Eat	27
7	The Plague of Men-Only Leadership Teams	29
8	Beyond Giving Women a Voice	33
9	Calling Female Refugee Workers to Life	39
10	The Wife's Voice and the Truth About Sex: Part One	41
11	The Wife's Voice and the Truth About Sex: Part Two	49
12	The Voice of Beauty	55
13	What's a Woman to Do?	59
14	Forbidden Leadership	67
15	Two More Items of Concern	69
	In Closing	73
	Two Additional Resources	75

… 1 …

A Lesser Species?

As believers in Christ Jesus, we all know there are various levels of created beings. We know that God created man and that God created angels, but angels were not created in God's image and are therefore inferior to man.

But did you know that there is another level of creation between man and angels?

Women.

Most of you reading this may be horrified to read this. Perhaps all of you would disagree with it.

My problem with certain people and church cultures in the body of Christ is that there are those who would adamantly, in their words, disagree that women are a lesser species but live as if it were true.

In the region where I live and in my travels as a speaker, I have become increasingly aware of how men diminish women in the following areas:

- Men in leadership roles who ignore feminine influence.
- Husbands who keep the glory of their wives in a tiny box by embracing a flawed perspective of submission and headship in the home.
- Religious movements that believe hiding a woman's beauty is virtuous.

- Cultures that define sexuality in male terms.

In this book I'll address two issues that are misaligned with the heart of God:

1. Men who dominate women.
2. Women who surrender to it.

I must say before I go further that those of you who are guilty of what I just noted may be guilty not because you have a depraved heart. Some may. But I realize that many of you, both men and women, are only acting out of what you were taught to be right. If that is the case with you, my hope is that this short book can change your mind about a woman's role in the kingdom of God. It is to you I write this book, not as an accuser, not as a finger-pointing judge, but as a father in the kingdom who wants you to see a more excellent way.

One of the audiences I'm writing to is the conservative, rule-based religions that have spread out across the United States over the past decades. Ruthie and I often grieve over how women in these cultures are taught and forced to live.

Recently a very mature woman from a conservative religious culture, after listening to one of my teachings on my Bruce Lengeman YouTube channel, "Master vs. Father" wrote the following to me:

> I feel sad that so many of our ladies' voices have been silenced and that so many have lived with the assumption that it's the right, godly, and scriptural thing to do. I've been growing in bringing my voice, and not just with my husband. I want more growth in bringing my voice with confidence, wisdom, and respect wherever I have an influence. Contending for my voice has been and still is a countercultural and sometimes difficult climb. Or...is it a humble descent to the cross?

> I really appreciate that our lead pastor wants all the pastors' wives present at their monthly meeting because he invites and values feminine input. There's something about the Genesis 3 curse on Satan (the enmity between the serpent and the woman) that speaks of the influence the enemy knows that women have, that he wants to keep veiled, covered, and hidden.
>
> It feels mysterious somehow, and I don't understand it all, but it feels powerful to me—the influence of a woman. There's glory connected to that! Right?
>
> In your "Master vs. Father" video teaching, I like the way you called out these [male dominated] groups by telling them that they need feminine input! Thank you!

Let's explore what's behind the idea that the influence of women is inferior to that of men. But first let's examine some things you must understand before we go further.

2

7 Essential Points That Will Help You Understand the Focus of *Voice!*

As the subhead of this book conveys, the theme of *Voice!* is *restoring the heart and influence of women in marriage, church, leadership, sexuality, and life...without sabotaging the dignity of men!* Decades of experience alert me to the kind of questions that may pop up in the minds of some of those reading *Voice!* I realized that I could evade those questions or challenges and defend the focus of this book in two ways. The first way is by embellishing this book with over-explaining each concept. The result would be a book four times the length I envisioned. Some books are more sensitive and delicate to write. This is one of them.

After I published my book on conquering sexual dependency at the root, *To Kill a Lion*, some people pointed out that I could have explained this or that concept more. One young woman who reviewed the pre-publishing manuscript of *Voice!* suggested I expand on a certain point in the book. What I usually say to this is "I could embellish every point in this book, but nobody wants to read a thousand-page book." So some of the "figuring out" of the things I didn't write has to be up to you, the reader.

The other way to deflect those questions, the one I chose, is *to head them off at the pass* by addressing them here, in the beginning, in just a few pages. Here are seven points that will enable you to understand my focus in *Voice!*

1. Not Addressing the Other Side—Men Are Guilty Too!

It's often said that there are two sides to every story. Writing a book from the viewpoint of only one side is very challenging. I didn't want to create another male-bashing book, although I felt compelled to confront a problem in male-female relationships writing on behalf of the female. Ruthie is presently writing a book on behalf of the male viewpoint, which when published may create a broader picture. *Voice!* is crafted only to address a serious and extensive social-relational problem—*devaluing the influence of women.*

I'm not naïve enough to think after five decades in the people-helping arena that women aren't also guilty of devaluing a man's voice. In certain environments the male voice is devalued, and women are often domineering too. But my focus in this book is to come alongside the female gender—hoping to give both women and men understanding, wisdom, and strategy to conquer a prevalent attitude among men who claim to follow Christ yet squelch the human equality of women.

2. Not Negating Male Leadership

Nothing of what I write negates the idea of male leadership in the home. Healthy, godly leadership in any arena does not devalue those who follow. Contrary to the beliefs of some, kingdom leadership is not dominating. Jesus taught the opposite—*the greatest leaders are the greatest servants.* So my goal in *Voice!* is to expose what I believe to be the perversions of how people view and treat women. I will also address flawed theology among certain religious groups that creates a style of "submission" for women that God never intended.

Though I believe the Creator designed men for leadership far more than women, I do not think that men are always the best leaders. The predominance of male leadership in the world and in marriage is not a social construct (created by social conditioning). It is also not just a theological construct. Male leadership is neurological (brain), it is chemical (estrogen vs. testosterone, and more), it is biological (DNA), and it is historical (sociological history repeatedly reflects that predominant male leadership is not socially determined). To believe that women carry the same universal tendency to lead is naïve.

In all my years of counseling, Ruthie and I have never had a man express a longing for his wife to lead the home better, but commonly—as in *continuously*—we hear the cry of women longing for their husbands to rise up and lead. Conversely, history has also birthed multitudes of great women leaders who rank equal to or higher than some great male leaders. I know there are legitimate exceptions to male leadership . I served under a female pastor—an amazing one. The churches I have pastored have been largely made up of married couples. The women do not have an inferior voice on those teams. At one of the churches I presently oversee there are two single women on the leadership team who share the same authority as the men. Yet a large initiative in my conferences for men is challenging men to rise up, take courage, access their God-identity, and lead. This leads to the next point.

3. Not Promoting *Equal Voice in All Things*

This may sound contradictory, but *equal value* does not always mean your voice will carry as much influence as somebody else's. When somebody is a leader in a business, a church, a family, or a team, that leader's voice carries a heavier weight, a more significant influence. In my marriage I am the clear leader. For the most part, Ruthie and I co-lead, but I carry the primary vision for the direction of the home. On the other hand, there are tons of times I know Ruthie is gifted with keys to our forward motion, steps to what we need to do, puzzle pieces to our success as a family, that I don't have. In these cases my voice is not as influential as hers, but I am not devalued in that process, the same as the fact that when I lead she is not devalued. This is the way we work as a healthy team. I'm not big enough to say there are not exceptions to predominant male leadership in the home—I'm sure there are—but in general they are not the default perspective.

Let me give you two examples to clarify what I just wrote: In my ministry duties and decisions, I would freak out if I had to run everything by Ruthie. I make many exclusive decisions about the forward motion of our ministry engagements. But there are places within our ministry career that I defer to Ruthie. *Defer* means "to humbly, voluntarily, and respectfully submit." An example: Ruthie and I are highly involved in active hospitality. Whenever Ruthie and I have a difference of opinion on something related to hospitality, I defer to Ruthie—that is her territory. I cook most of the meals when we host somebody, but I always acknowledge that when it comes to hosting, I submit to her—gladly!

4. Not Primarily a Rebuke

My intention in this book is not to extend a harsh rebuke to men or to women. If what I write exposes something flawed in your beliefs or behaviors, then I say, *If the shoe fits, wear it!* But I write this to expose lies to those of you who may not even know you've made agreements with beliefs that are out of alignment with the intentions of the Creator. This book is to help those of you who seek truth in this area of concern.

5. Not Addressing Petty Disagreements

I'm aware that there may be a tendency with some to over-apply the principles in this book. I am not concerned about typical disagreements that happen in life due to personality, value, culture, and style diversity. In this book I address *a universal mentality—a behavioral pattern* that devalues women. I am certainly not saying that women should always *get their way* on committees, teams, in marriage, or at work. So please be careful not to over-implement the principles in this book in situations of normal relational disagreements and challenges.

6. Not Saying that a Woman Does Not Have a Respected Voice

A woman's or a wife's influence may not be respected, due not to a man devaluing her equality but rather because she may have behavioral, emotional, or spiritual *issues*—obstacles in her heart that need healed, or self-preservation filters through which she views life. As a counselor, mentor, pastor, husband, person, I'm aware of this. Women, don't blame men who don't respect you if you live and talk through flawed paradigms of life.

7. Not a Flaky Feminist Book

This book has nothing to do with the feminist movement. Though some of what I say may be similar to a few points made by feminists, contemporary feminism is also a movement that devalues the Creator's design for women. I am not writing this to say to every woman, *You are enough*, or to echo Helen Reddy in her hit song, *If I have to, I can do anything. I am strong, I am invincible, I am woman*. I am simply writing to teach the equal human value of women as per God's design and what that means in society and in a woman's life.

So please keep these seven perspectives in mind as you read *Voice!* lest you misrepresent my heart or miss the truth being taught.

3

Screwed-Up Theology and the Glory of an Ezer

Throughout the gospels Jesus broke accepted paradigms and practices by saying in essence, *"You may have heard it said, but I say..."* I believe one of the practices that Jesus is breaking today is the *devaluing of woman*.

To understand the theology of women in our world, a few defining principles will clarify God's perspective of a woman's value on earth.

The Amazing Revelation of a Misunderstood Hebrew Word

God created woman out of man. "So God created man in His own image; in the image of God He created him; male and female He created them" (Genesis 1:27). He took a rib, a bone out of the man's side. He didn't take a bone out of the man's heel. Woman was designed to walk alongside a man—equal in value yet different in her "role."

"And the Lord God said, *'It is not good that man should be alone; I will make him a helper comparable to him'*" (Genesis 2:18). The Hebrew word for *helper comparable* (or suitable helper or help meet) is the word *ezer*. Let me show you something about the word *ezer* that may rock what you may have always believed about the woman being a *help meet*.

I looked up all twenty-one times *ezer* appears in the Bible. Twice *ezer* refers to "woman" (Eve) and sixteen of the remaining times, *ezer* refers to God—as an *ezer* to His people! That says something incredibly significant about women. Woman to man is like God to His people. He is more than just a *help meet*. One Hebrew scholar says *ezer* should have been translated "sustainer alongside." Help meet communicates the idea of *lesser in value, subservient*, which is not what *ezer* means.

Ponder these verses in relation to what God said about the woman he created for Adam.

> He is your shield and helper [*ezer*] and your glorious sword. (Deuteronomy 33:29, KJV)

> I lift up my eyes to the hills—from whence comes my help [*ezer*]? My help [*ezer*] comes from the Lord, who made heaven and earth. (Psalm 121:1–2)

> We wait in hope for the Lord; he is our help [*ezer*] and our shield. (Psalm 33:20)

A better translation, therefore, of *ezer* would be "lifesaver."

Ruthie, My *Ezer*

Does it stun you that I refer to Ruthie as my *ezer*? I am the clear head of my home even in the light of my saying that *Ruthie and I co-lead our home!* Ruthie loves my leadership! No contradiction. Ruthie respects my leadership, but...

Ruthie has a valuable and respected voice in almost every weighty decision I make—or should I say that we make. Therefore, Ruthie loves my leadership and undergirds it, but most of the time we are co leading.

Every aspect of what she feels about anything we do is safely a part of our oneness. Throughout the rest of this book I want to expound on what this oneness looks like.

A More Significant Voice

Ruthie not only has a voice in the decisions we make, *but she also has a voice in my life, how I live, and how I relate to others.* I didn't say she *controls* these things—I said she has a voice. Therefore, I can honestly say that Ruthie has influenced my life more than any book, more than any friend, more than any spiritual leader. Oh, God forbid where I would be if I had accepted a common view that women's influence and opinion are inferior!

Ruthie has been a God-*ezer* in my life—through Ruthie God speaks His will to me and gives me life, direction, and affirmation (to me through Ruthie)! Continuously what she thinks and feels is more "right, accurate, God's heart" than what I may think or feel myself.

Ruthie has helped me avoid mistakes and even failures. She has motivated me to be sensitive to people in cases in which I would have been insensitive—even wounded people. She has opened the door for me, and us, to do things that I didn't want to do but ended up amazing. I benefited by submitting and supporting her heart. She has heard from God in instances when God didn't speak to me but to her. This brought life to both of us. She has contended for necessary changes in my life that I didn't see were needed, but because I released her to speak into my life, I'm a better person for taking the time to see what Ruthie sees. And she speaks those things to me without making me feel disrespected or inadequate. Ruthie's belief in my *better self* makes me feel like her king!

Not only has Ruthie enhanced my life as an *ezer*, but she has also been an equal contributor to our forward motion in life and our ministry success. She has solved problems that have confronted us in a way I never could have. There were many times Ruthie had a strong opinion on how to deal with an issue, an opinion that I disagreed with but in which in my heart I perceived that God was speaking to me through her. In those times I had to *die to my own opinions* and value what God was saying through her. Inevitably I returned to her and thanked her for using her voice, and I thanked God for giving me wisdom to listen to her because she had keys that I didn't.

―――――― 4 ――――――

The "Lesser Woman" Concept Revealed at a Couples' Meeting

Ruthie and I were asked to speak at a couples' get-together of people who had grown up in very conservative and strict religious cultures but were seeking a fresh look at life beyond religion. They were amazing people, hungry for truth.

The host gave every couple a different question about marriage. We went around in a circle, each couple assigned to answer the question that was on the table in front of them. Out of the twenty couples there, at least sixteen of the questions were answered by the husband. Ruthie and I were stunned that so many of the men neglected to say, "Honey, how would you answer this?" I sensed that the couples present never even noticed what Ruthie and I noticed, since most of them had grown up in a religious culture that didn't value the female voice.

A few days later I mentioned this to the primary leader. He hadn't noticed, but he cared. He is a leader who passionately desires to live life, to live marriage, God's way.

Don't Challenge the Leader!

The situation I'm about to relate to you is true and accurate in detail. But it's only one situation of many I could tell you about. Names have been changed to protect the guilty.

Darvin was the pastor. He, like many other pastors and leaders whom I was aware of or worked with, would make critical decisions independent of the advice of his team, decisions that ought to have been made *with* his team, because those decisions *affected* the team. And because of his independence, his decisions *infected* his team. Many of the decisions he made had negative consequences. Some of them worked, but he left behind him a trail of resentful subjects. The church was full of mature, wise people—leaders in their own arenas. But time and time and time again I would observe or hear about decisions Darvin would make that were insensitive, unwise, not planned well, and so forth, but the team and the people of the church sat passively by on the grounds that *Darvin is the leader—we should not challenge him*, though inside they felt abused. I loved Darvin. He was a highly effective leader. But most *Darvins* in time lose respect.

Another thing I noticed about Darvin is that he rarely gave his wife a chance to voice her opinions on his decisions. I knew that his wife could have and would have saved Darvin from countless inferior decisions, but instead, his wife did not think it was her place to challenge the authority of her leader/husband, husband/pastor. In the process his wife devalued the importance of her own voice—*Who am I to think I could, or should, influence my leader-husband?* So therefore the man in such a situation goes on misaligned to the heart of God, living inadequately because his life is not aligned with the heart of his wife. That does not mean that he isn't successful. But *success* and *kingdom* are not synonyms. Trillions of initiatives have been successful but are far from being God-authored. Never be blinded or deceived by success!

Women Hear from God as Much as Men!

I understand leadership. I sometimes make decisions despite contrary opinions when I as a leader sense that I am following God's leading. But I know, believe, and access the truth that Ruthie hears from

God every bit as much as me. She knows, though, and respects that I have a *leadership* impartation that she hasn't been graced with. Often Ruthie perceives *more* than me, and my leadership role is to discern that my best option is to listen to and move with what *Ruthie* is sensing, not what *I* sense. Ruthie's *voice* has been the blessed key to multitudes of different situations and challenges that have confronted us.

The First Chapter Tells It

To quote again Genesis 1:27, "In the image of God He created him; male and female He created them." He created *them*, male and female—equal, co-valuable. But then, noted four times in the Bible, the two shall become *one flesh* (Genesis 2:24; Matthew 19:5; Mark 10:8; Ephesians 5:31). How can two become one when one of the two demeans the other's value in the relationship?

Is God Male? Is He Allah?

God made male and female to display—together—the fullness of who God is. Does God have only testosterone traits? Are you kidding me? No! God has all good traits. Many religious groups might as well call themselves Muslims regarding their attitude toward women. In many dominant sections of Islam, women are subservient. They are treated with less God-value than men. I know men who would scoff at Muslims for their view of women but then embrace the same putrid, religious attitude toward their own wives.

I have found that when men wake up and discover a deep relationship with the Holy Spirit of Christ, one of the first things they often do is start valuing their wives and other women, giving them the voice they never had before.

---- 5 ----

Whatever Happened to Verse 21?

I was helping to officiate a marriage ceremony in Greece. In my wedding challenge I talked about the most frequently quoted passage of the Bible at wedding ceremonies, Ephesians 5. Everyone that I have ever heard use this scripture begins at verse 22: "Wives, submit to your own husbands." And then, of course, it progresses to verse 25: "Husbands, love your wives." At the wedding I said, "But the passage doesn't begin at verse 22! It begins at verse 21: "Submitting to one another in the fear of God." There is a pungent phrase embellishing that command, 'in the fear of God.' *Submitting yourselves one to another* is not an option in marriage—it is a command. Men who demean their wives may have a *happy* marriage, but they don't have a *kingdom* marriage."

After the ceremony in Greece, one of the relatives approached me and said, "You're the first person I ever heard say what I believe about the importance of verse 21!"

The Verse on the Cover

The verse on the cover of this book is likely the most significant affirmation of what I'm writing about:

There is neither Jew nor Greek, there is neither slave nor

free, there is neither male nor female; for you are all one in Christ Jesus. (Galatians 3:28)

Though I believe women can and do excel in God being primary leaders in churches, businesses, and other organizations, I do not deny that universally and historically, even in remote places isolated from the influence of civilized humankind, men rise to leadership far more than women in almost every culture that has ever been. It is not cultural—it is biological. Yet who can deny the leadership potential of women? We have no qualms about women being on our leadership teams. Many years ago when I was the pastor of a church, we were part of a family of churches. One of the most significant churches had a female pastor—an amazing female leader. She led the way in that church as few men could.

You may disagree with me, but the leadership teams I have had the privilege of overseeing have benefited beyond words by having women on them. I'm passionate about releasing women to be all God made them to be. I do not persuade all believers to take the same stand that I do with women in leadership, but what I am adamant about is that *without the influence of women, leaders will never discern the fullness of the heart of God. To do that, you need the female voice, however you tap into it!*

6

I Know It's True When We Go Out to Eat

Multiple times—too many times--Ruthie and I have been with leaders who, in my words, *give testimony of themselves*. They are perpetually talking about their own agendas, expressing their own hearts, talking about all the things God is doing—in their own personal ministries and lives. They spew knowledge. They interrupt. They teach. They dominate conversation. But what I am perturbed about is the way these leaders ignore their wives.

Allow me to describe one situation that represents countless similar situations. I met up with a leader who dominated most of our time together talking. But more, he never turned to his wife and asked, "Honey, what are you thinking?" I certainly don't want to toot my own horn, but honestly, I can't imagine a social conversation in which I don't open the door for Ruthie to talk at the same level as me! In every social encounter—at a restaurant or at somebody's home—I will always say multiple times, "Ruthie, what are you thinking?"

Regularly, not rarely, we come home from meetings with leaders who tsunami us in conversation and never, ever say to the female beside them, *"Honey, what would you say?"* So when we are with those people, Ruthie is always directing the conversation to the wife by asking her the questions her husband never would. I've learned with certain people that I have to say what I want to say in fifteen seconds or less before they interrupt with their own ideas, thoughts, and opinions. This is not esteeming others as more important than yourself (Philippians 2:3). It is narcissistic.

7

The Plague of Men-Only Leadership Teams

Honestly, I'm not going to challenge you if you think that only men should be on leadership teams. (That's not saying that I agree with that view.) But the perversion (I chose that word because that's the best word to describe what I'm about to say) of male leadership teams is thinking that they don't need the insight, wisdom, and heart of women. When you have only an all-male perspective, you have only a "half-God" perspective. Male leadership teams operating solely without the God- heart of women may succeed, but they rarely succeed in kingdom terms. Only what God is the *author and finisher* of will stand at the final judgment.

Consulting with a Ministry

One of my primary roles is organizational consulting. I was hired to consult with an organization that had an international ministry but was struggling with direction. After a couple of sessions and several hours, I realized their lack. One of the members of the board asked me, *What is your advice to reconcile some of these issues?*

I answered with something I perceive they didn't like and something they didn't do. I said, "In this ministry you' re seriously missing the female perspective. I'm not asking you to put women on your board, but if you don't tap into female wisdom, you'll suffer without it!"

I was never asked back.

Comment from an Elder's Wife

"The main argument I have heard from my parents and other people who believe in male-only leadership teams is that women need to be protected from some of the harder conversations and decisions in church leadership. They say that they are too weak and emotional to handle the pressure of leadership. Of course, I had to fight against that lie when Dean became an elder, because that lie is what I was taught by my parents and the religious culture I was brought up in.

I think often about the weight my voice now carries with Dean—how he pays attention more to my feedback than anyone else's. It's almost an unspoken deference and posture of the heart for him. How do you teach a man to make that transition if it has not always been that way? It takes both spouses to come to that place—the woman to rise and realize the power and value of her words, and the man to receive and take to heart what she is saying. I know the power of my words to Dean is sobering, so I make sure what I am sharing is coming from a godly motive, especially at times that I may bring a correction to him. It is in the sin nature of a woman to criticize and not freely give respect to her husband until he has 'earned' it. When women realize they have more voice, it needs to be weighed carefully, and it cannot be used as an excuse to shoot him down over every failure."

I Don't Know Who Wrote It, but It's Good!

I don't know who wrote the following, but I got it from wordimpartation.com:

God created both man and woman in the image of God. Jesus is equal to the Father but chose to submit to the Father and become our Savior. The Holy Spirit is equal to the Father and to Jesus, yet the Holy Spirit points us to Jesus and is our Helper—with us and in us (John 14:16). The Three-in-One exhibit no rivalry, competition, or inferiority but are co-equal and fully God, working together to accomplish God's will and plan. Marriage between a man and a woman is to model that kind of love. God's creation from Adam's rib brought forth a suitable helper who was equal, opposite to, and together they became one flesh.

8

Beyond Giving Women a Voice

In general terms, our society does not equip men to undergird and support the hearts of women. Marriages fail often because many husbands are clueless as to what it means to nurture a woman's heart. But for a moment let me explain something you would likely hear if you came to a marriage seminar taught by Ruthie and me, or our *Releasing Life in Your Church* workshop—we refer to it as *calling to life*.

In the churches I oversee, everybody must know what *calling to life* means. It is the heart and soul of our spiritual family. *Calling to life* happens when somebody sees a more excellent way a person could be living and helps him or her to understand it. *Calling to life* happens when Ruthie sees in me an authority that I don't see, and she helps me to understand it. *Calling to life* happens when I see God's heart for somebody that he or she doesn't see and I help the person understand it. *Calling to life* happens when you share hope with somebody when he or she has little hope and you help him or her understand it. *Calling to life* happens when you see someone caught in error or sin and you speak the truth and help the person understand it.

One of my most important actions as a shepherd is to call people to life.

One of my most important privileges as a husband is to call Ruthie to life.

VOICE!

I wrote the following poem to express what *calling to life* is:

*"I saw an angel
in the marble
then carved until
I set her free"—
a quote by
Michelangelo
but those same
eyes
I want
for me.
Lo, we all are
rough, unformed,
we all are
undefined,
but love sees
something deeper
where commonly
we're blind.
Oh, to have the eyes
to see
what eludes the
average man.
Oh, to help
a piece of rock
embrace a finer,
more glorious
plan.
For they
cannot themselves
perceive*

*the angel locked
inside
of the hope
of something great that
has
faded,
disappeared,
or died.
Let me use a chisel,
Lord,
where You created
more.
Grace me
as an artist
to reveal
an angel's core.
Let me see in others
the majesty
hidden away.
Give me, Lord,
the skill to free
their masterpiece
to display.
"I saw an angel
in the marble
then carved until
I set her free."
Oh, what eyes
what piercing eyes,
but those are eyes
I want
for me.*

In our marriage workshops, Ruthie often says that this is what I did for her–release the angel within. But I follow telling the audience that Ruthie did the same for me!

Ruthie is powerful. Nobody who knows her would disagree. Her voice is loved, respected, and sought after in every environment we are in. Ruthie is a mother to younger women, a mentor to peers, and co-teaches in most of the workshops, seminars, and meetings we are invited to. But there is something you might not know about Ruthie.

When Ruthie and I were dating, we would have devotions daily, studying the Bible, talking about life, praying. One day after I shared an insight with her, I asked her, *Ruthie, what do you think?* I didn't find out till years later what went on inside Ruthie's mind when I asked her that question. She panicked! She had no idea of what to say. She so devalued her opinion and so respected mine that she literally had nothing to say to answer my question.

Ruthie often refers to that in her *identity* teachings. She is no longer that same girl who doesn't have confidence in her voice, her opinions, her perspectives. She is outspoken, confident, and tremendously influential. Believe me—she has lots to say now. Praise God!

Reflections from Ruthie:

When people ask me, What enabled you to change? I answer, Bruce saw the angel in the rock and carved until he set me free. It was often not a pleasant experience, but I thank God that I have a husband who loved me enough to take me where my flesh didn't want to go!

The first time I read this manuscript I noticed right away how much Bruce used my name throughout. I felt honored and valued. The things he wrote in this book he has lived all our married lives. *We have had to work hard at it. It hasn't always been easy,* but the time and tears it took to get here have all been so worth it! We are more in love now than we were forty-five years ago—and I truly mean that! I deeply bless Bruce for the value he has placed in my life and the places he has refused to allow me to think less of myself than what God thinks. In the value he has poured into my life, it is with joy that I serve alongside Bruce!

9

Calling Female Refugee Workers to Life

I had the privilege of being asked to speak on a Sunday morning to all the staff and volunteers of a humanitarian ministry that worked in a massive refugee camp in Greece. For several days before Sunday, I was seeking God about what I should speak on, but I got nothing—*nada*! On Sunday morning I got up early and trekked a short few hundred feet to a café on the water, where I sat hoping to get my "word" from God. While there, I made a list of five things I thought might be relevant to share about.

Little did I know that God was ignoring my notes.

I arrived at the meeting room for the service and took a seat near the rear where the chairs were for the older staff and couples. The others, mostly young adults, sat on the floor against the walls surrounding the worship leader. No sooner had I sat down than the Lord said to me, *Call the women to life.*

The women were dressed like many people in my home county, Lancaster Pennsylvania—head coverings, dresses well below the knees, mostly styled in a very religiously conservative fashion. Having worked intensely with the Amish and Mennonite culture over my past three decades of ministry, I understood that many of the girls in that group came from churches that depreciate a woman's voice and teach women to be subservient to men. In word, but not action, men would call women equals—but it's often sounds more like an Allah perspective than a Jehovah one.

I knew only a few people in the group, and the ones I did know I had just met the past few days since I arrived. When it was my time to speak after an amazing time of worship, I started in on the women—addressing lies about women and teaching them what it meant to rise to their God-identity. It was not a challenge to *rise up, shake your fist, and assert yourself.* It simply was a challenge to confront the devil's lies about who they were designed to be. I pointed out that God had shown me that many of them had quenched their thoughts, made agreements with Satan's devaluation of them, and that God wanted to set them free today. I told them that they do indeed hear from God and that their voice is needed, valued, and powerful.

It was as if I were drilling a well and hit a geyser—the young girls and several of the older didn't hesitate to come to the front at my invitation to renounce lies they had embraced about their identity in Christ. Tissues were needed from the east side of the room to the west. I was hoping I hadn't violated the values of that group—I never want to do that wherever I speak, but I knew what God had told me to do.

Later that day and the next, I got feedback from two of the leaders that something broke at that meeting. They had just started meeting together since some of the COVID requirements were lifted, but the leaders were sensing something had been hindering the spiritual atmosphere. Something wasn't clicking. Whatever wasn't clicking was broken at that meeting, according to those leaders and testimonials that I heard a few weeks later.

Wherever and whenever the influence and voice of women are quenched, *something will be out of alignment!* In Christ there is no male nor female—as far as value and significance are concerned.

10

The Wife's Voice and the Truth About Sex: Part One

The subtitle of this book is *restoring the heart and influence of women in marriage, church, leadership, sexuality, and life!* Because *sexuality* is a subtopic of marriage, I could have chosen not to list it in the subtitle. But though it is a subtopic of marriage, it is also a major issue that deserves its own specific treatment. I perceived that listing *sexuality* in the subtitle would attract women who feel sexually dominated in their marriage.

For many decades Ruthie and I have been teaching Christian couples the truths about a healthy, fulfilling, Godly sex life. We do it in our counseling, our seminars, and our pre-marital courses. Our course, *Sexuality and Intimacy in Marriage*, is a revelation for many who have never been taught what healthy sex in marriage looks and feels like.

The sad truth is that a healthy sexual culture among believers seems to be more *an exception than the rule*.

Though Ruthie and I understand that the reasons for couples having an unhealthy sex life are not just the fault of men—women are often major contributors to unhealthy sex in marriage. But as I mentioned at the very beginning of this book, what I am writing is designed to restore a woman's voice in the bedroom. We have other written material that covers the man's back—or front, whatever!

Perspective from Ruthie

In our many roles as people helpers, especially counseling married couples, Bruce and I have discovered that multitudes of Christian wives don't enjoy sex because their husbands have created a sexual culture in their marriages that fulfills **him** but does not fulfill **her**. Her voice in the bedroom is neglected or shut down. She then feels like no more than a toy, an object, or a faithful, submissive wife created to be a sexual slave so her hubby can have his orgasm.

Bruce and I have a wonderful sex life. We've had to work at it and work at it diligently. "Work at it" means that I had to learn what fulfills Bruce in the context of healthy sex, and he had to learn my wants and needs. We taught each other about our sexual wants and needs. Both of us desire the best for the other in sex. Bruce has never once in our whole marriage forced me to have sex when I couldn't enter in with my heart; he never put me on a guilt trip if I was too tired, not feeling well, or was fighting the kind of emotions a mother has—especially at night. He never even got frustrated with me. There were times we had some unfulfilled desires in the bedroom, but only as it was part of our journey learning the wisdom of a marriage relationship.

The best way I can communicate a woman's voice in the bedroom is to elaborate on a few of the principles Bruce and I teach in our Sexuality and Intimacy in Marriage seminar.

Worship:

Friends of Lisa and Mark (not real names) dragged them to one of our marriage workshops after they found out that they were planning to get divorced. They had two children. At our workshop they decided to give it one more chance, that is, *if* Bruce and I would counsel them.

It worked. Today they have a healthy marriage. But shortly after the restoration process began, they attended a weekend *Sexuality and Intimacy in Marriage* seminar that Bruce and I taught. We began by calling the sexual relationship *worship*. We explained what that meant—that sex in marriage is more than an outlet for sexual feelings, but it is also an act of worship the same as when we sit on the couch or lie in bed together in the morning and pray.

Lisa and Mark were late for the Saturday morning breakfast. Halfway through breakfast they joined us. Their excuse for being late was, *we were worshiping*. We laughed, but that's when their third child was conceived—in an act of worship.

Intimacy:

When you have *intimacy* sex—or said another way, when intimacy and sex are intertwined so that they become the same thing—you realize how cheap sex without oneness and intimacy is.

Intimacy in sex means that Bruce's and my heart are *connecting* as much as our bodies are. It is the essence of "making love." Sadly, too many Christian couples have sex but don't *make love*. Bruce wrote a book titled *Come Alive to Her Heart: A Challenge for Married Men on Emotional Connecting*. He wrote it because repeatedly in the counseling room we hear the troubled hearts of women married to men who have never been taught how to hold the hearts of their wives. Our culture doesn't teach it, many fathers and mothers don't know it, so they can't teach it to their children, and flawed theology teaches a warped version of it. I don't have the space to elaborate here on all the things in *Come Alive*, but it is a great follow-up book for couples to this book you are reading.

Intimacy in sex means that our sexual union is a celebration of the fun, the life, the love, the oneness, the communion with God that we share 24/7. That makes sex a wonderful experience for both of us. One of the terms we use to describe what we do in sex is *emotionalizing*. It means that in sex we make the other feel loved, feel celebrated, and feel good!

Bruce had to learn that many women, I being one, are not as "orgasm oriented" as a man. In general, for the man the *orgasm* is the *climax*. But for most women, though they may enjoy an orgasm, the orgasm is not the climax—*the climax is the whole emotional, sexual, all-day experience.* One of Bruce's personal mentors in marriage counseling, a professor at college, used to say about women, "Great sex at night begins with a goodbye kiss in the morning." For most women it is impossible to compartmentalize sex—to detach it from a whole-life experience. If a woman doesn't feel as if her heart is held by her husband, she may never be able to enter into sex with her whole heart.

Oneness:

Everything I've written in this chapter falls under the category of one flesh. The Bible tells us, "They [the husband and wife] become one flesh" (Genesis 2:24). *Oneness* in marital sexuality releases intimacy and a vibrant expression of love.

Defining Sex:

What is sex to the wife, and what is sex to the husband? Our culture defines sex in male terms—it always has. If a woman's sexuality is a square peg and a man's is a round hole, defining sexuality in male terms is like trying to put a square peg in a round hole. It doesn't work!

My Voice:

Far more than women, men are guilty of bringing *lust* into marriage. Bruce and I are not legalists when it comes to rules for godly sex. But taking immoral lustful drives and translating them into marriage is unhealthy. Sometimes couples don't know the difference and may need counsel on the heart issues that may be detracting from an intimate sex life. To be honest, Bruce and I had to work through some of those issues. (He describes his sexual journey in his book *To Kill a Lion*.) I will relate an incident (of many) that illustrates how Bruce gives me a voice. After a few years of marriage, I told Bruce that I felt an intimacy

A WIFE'S VOICE AND THE TRUTH ABOUT SEX: PART ONE

disconnect with a certain way, a very minor practice, in which we would sometimes express ourselves sexually. That's all I had to say, and we never did it again. Bruce will declare truthfully that he never regretted or missed expressing ourselves that way. He was more concerned that we were always *making love*. What we were expressing was absolutely not sin or *kinky*, but for me that practice that happened every now and then wasn't emotionally desired.

One of my most sexual times is when Bruce and I sit on the couch and watch a movie. He always puts his arm across me. I feel so secure, protected, and loved. I crave watching movies with Bruce because I love the sexual feeling of Bruce *making love* to me this way. It is very sexual in my way—closeness, warmth, a secure time!

Another example was when I told Bruce I needed some "let down" time before heading to the bedroom. Bruce, like most men, could disengage from the duties of the day better than I could. And I didn't want Bruce to be another thing I *checked off my list* before going to sleep. It was years into our marriage when I sat down and told him about my need to chill and let down before we headed to the bedroom. Without any challenge to my need, Bruce made sure I had that time to read, watch the news, talk about the day, or whatever. Now all nine children are married, and Bruce is still making sure I have that *let down time* when I need it. It doesn't have to be a long time or every night. Sometimes I need only a few minutes.

Girls, your voice in sex is as important as your husband's. Hopefully what I have written here in this chapter will help you to understand truth, but also to **value your own desires and needs in the sexual arena**. Recently a woman who had been married several decades commented to us that her desire for sex was failing. She said, "I guess that's what happens when you get older." Bruce told me later that he sensed that her lack of desire for sex had nothing to do with age but rather that she was missing the main ingredient in her sexual experience—intimacy with her husband.

45

The Perfect Plan:

I love sex with Bruce. I love his male sexuality, and he loves my female sexuality. Each has unique but different motivations. Bruce often teaches that the way the Lord designed female sexually is exactly what a man needs and wants and that the way He designed male sexuality is exactly what a woman needs and wants. But this is realized and experienced only within the contexts of true love, genuine giving to one another, abundant intimacy, and heart-to-heart connecting. God didn't make a mistake by making us different—He blessed us!

Exclusivity:

Women need to feel exclusive. This is often the place women lose their voice and suffer emotionally. *Exclusivity* means that at all times, in every situation, she knows that she is the most important focus of her husband's life. Bruce had to travel when we were raising children. Though we were apart, he always made sure he called me every day, and usually several times a day. Even though he was busy and had to deal with his career and duties of life, I never felt second to his career. Bruce would never flirt with another woman, would never talk to another woman about heart issues without my being present, would never go to lunch with a female work partner without me. **This knowledge in my heart keeps me open to all the love-making Bruce and I do.** Women can also be very *possessive* out of insecurity. For a man to give a wife exclusivity doesn't mean he has to become co dependent to her wounds and weaknesses. It is simply couples valuing the core focus of their marriage covenant—*and the two shall become one!*

Pornography:

A man who indulges in porn violates himself, God, and his wife. A wife will never feel exclusive while her husband is lusting at other women. A wife needs to know that she alone is *enough* for her husband. A lifestyle of porn is never okay . It is never just a "male thing ." It is not to be excused based on *this is just what men do!* Mature, Godly men *don't!*

11

The Wife's Voice and the Truth About Sex: Part Two

When I Was Both Cursed and Blessed in Performing a Wedding Ceremony

Donna and Caleb asked me to include their final pre-marital counseling session as my address at their wedding ceremony. One of the things I mentioned in that address was the blessing of sex in marriage. I challenged them to maintain a foundation of intimacy that would enhance the glory of their sexual life.

The problem was that many of their relatives were from a very conservative church culture in which you don't mention the " s word" publicly or non-publicly. Talking about sex was a *no-no!*

It did not go over well with the relatives—*how inappropriate to talk about sex publicly! There were young people in the audience! How unholy!* My, oh, my—did it cause a stir! But on the other side, from those who were not of religious cultures, I got more accolades than I had ever received at a wedding: *That was the best wedding message I ever heard! Thanks for being so real!* And on and on. The pastor didn't speak to me and hardly even looked at me the rest of the night. No accolades from him or his wife.

You see, the problem with what happened at that wedding is that there was a general mentality among these religious conservatives that sex is *unholy*. Sex in marriage is a *necessary evil* but not something that you dare mention in a wedding ceremony or even talk to your children about.

I am wiser now after decades of working in ministry with people in conservative religious cultures. I understand the beliefs of those trapped in that flawed mindset.

I mentioned earlier in this book that some of what I am addressing in *Voice!* is directed to those who live in, or have come out of, a strict religious culture that demeans women. Lydia, a friend of ours, grew up in such a conservative culture. After her husband passed away, she found freedom from the sexual lies she had been taught in her church culture. One day Lydia texted me and asked if Ruthie and I would counsel her on some things she was bothered by. In our session with Lydia, she shared a horrific account of sexual abuse, both out of marriage and within her marriage. I asked her if she would share her experience for the book I was working on (*Voice!*) on how her voice in sexuality was ignored. Without a doubt, Lydia's testimonial is similar to the experience of many others in similar religious cultures.

Much of what Lydia shared with us during our counseling session included questions that emerged from a book she was reading, *The Great Sex Rescue*, by Sheila Wray Gregoire. I ordered a copy of it the next day. It is a brilliant challenge. The subtitle of the book is *The Lies You've Been Taught and How to Recover What God Intended*. Here is Lydia's testimonial.

Reflections from Lydia

As a young girl growing up in a very conservative religious culture, I heard a tremendous amount of teaching on *wives, submit to your husbands*. I had little respect for myself as a girl and a woman. My mother told me that prior to her own marriage, her mother told her that the honeymoon was not for sex and that she listened to her mother's advice. I chose not to listen to that advice, but it was the beginning of a sex life that was all about him and what he wanted and needed. Because *wives, submit yourselves to your husbands* was so deeply ingrained in our brains, I thought it was my duty to give him sex whenever he wanted. If he wanted sex three times a day, I submitted. My body was for him.

But we rarely ever did more than have sex. We rarely ever *made love!* He even felt guilty when he gave me sexual pleasure. So I went many years not knowing that I too was supposed to enjoy sex. When I did find out that I was supposed to have pleasure in sex, my husband did not want to go that far. Once somebody asked me if I ever said no to my husband when he wanted sex. I answered that I would rarely say *no*—I would just submit to all my husband's lustful desires. In those moments I felt totally worthless.

Once a church I had attended added a new rule to their church discipline: *Nobody may wear sandals.* I asked them *why*, and they answered, "Some of the men in leadership are turned on by women's feet, so they needed to be covered." I was so angry! The women in that church were being victimized because the men couldn't control their lust and wouldn't let God heal them!

When I was a young girl, it was conveyed to me that if I was sexually abused it was because I *"probably flirted, dressed immodestly, talked wrong, or invited it."* I grew up believing that I was responsible for the thoughts and actions of lustful men. I kept quiet about my sexual abuse.

Also, as stated earlier, I grew up thinking that I was supposed to sexually give my husband whatever he wanted. This thought is very prevalent in conservative settings. But I can't say for sure how widespread that thought is, because sex was something we were not allowed to talk about. The topic of sex was non-existent. As a child, when I would ask questions about sex, I would receive very shallow answers. I got yelled at once for watching a bull breed with a heifer behind the house.

So Sad!

Lydia's testimony is sad. The good part is that after the death of her husband, she began renouncing the lies she had been taught about sexuality and has now found much healing from the abuse she endured over many years of marriage. She is now a powerhouse for Jesus!

I would really love to devote a whole book to a comment by a counselor-friend named Veronica. She said, *"Women who've been abused before marriage are used to living under shame. It feels comfortable and familiar. It's easy to feel small, unimportant, and "less than." A Spirit-filled husband/pastor/leader/friend has the wonderful opportunity to be an effective aid in deep healing through proper affirmation and covering. I am grateful to have experienced this."*

Sexual abuse is one of the most difficult traumas to overcome, but God will give you *beauty for ashes*. Christ died on the cross to take our shame. When you live under sexual shame, it is very difficult to have a healthy mindset toward sex. Ask the Lord to remove the filter of shame through which you view life, and choose to reject the shameful thoughts that are designed to keep you feeling "not enough," "unclean," or "less than." Shame will motivate you to quench your voice, your influence, your significance, and your God-identity. Renounce shame and receive the *new creation* experience Jesus purchased for you!

A Sexuality Seminar among the Religious Conservative

I couldn't wait. Ruthie and I were asked to do a seminar for a ministry within a conservative religious community for those within who were hungry for truth. If I remember correctly, it involved about twenty-five couples. I knew most of those who attended were not used to talking about sex among themselves and definitely not accustomed to hearing it from the pulpit.

My First Session

In the first session I dove in full speed ahead. The topic was *Sex Is Good and Created by God as a Gift to His People*. I told them that " naked and not ashamed" in Genesis meant that modesty is not a part of a holy marriage. Modesty is an enemy to intimacy! I even talked about orgasms. *You wanna know about sex? I'm gonna tell ya!*

The response was overwhelmingly positive. The seminar climaxed (pun) with a sweetheart banquet. We went around in a circle and asked people to share what they had gotten from the seminar or anything else they would like to share about the weekend. The testimonies were amazing. But I'll never forget one of them. I'll change the names even though I probably don't have to.

Locked Out

Isaac and Esther told the story of one night after the kids were in bed when they decided to go out on the balcony in the raw. When they were out, they then realized that the door had locked behind them. By then we were all in stitches laughing! They tried figuring out how they were going to get back in. Isaac remembered that there was a key down by the barn, but to get there he had to enter the realm of the motion sensor light where he, in his raw state, would be highlighted for any neighbors to view. Alas, they were able to resolve their predicament. Isaac went for the run while asking God to temporarily blind the neighbors. But Isaac's and Esther's story freed the group to be open about talking about something that was not crude, not unholy, not vulgar, not indecent—marital sex!

12

The Voice of Beauty

Since the late 1980s, a huge part of my influence has been to those who would define themselves as *conservative Christians* and to those who *used to be* conservative. But worldwide there are multitudes of religious movements that many define as *conservative.* *Conservative* means something different in each different group, but I want to address what I believe to be a huge flaw in the thinking of almost every conservative group I have worked with or have observed throughout the world. That flaw is the sin of requiring girls and women to hide their beauty and teaching them that feeling beautiful, or wanting to feel beautiful, is unholy pride.

Men in conservative religions, for the most part, are able to blend into society without too much difference, but not women. They must hide a large part of the beauty their Creator endowed them with. I won't list all the ways the men in these religions keep their women un-beautiful, but I will address a flawed mindset that perpetuates this culture.

God made women to be beautiful, and no law, no rule, no "nothing" is going to take away the inner craving a woman has to feel beautiful. It is an organic process to want to be beautiful, because it was put into their hearts by God to feel beautiful. It is God's blessing in the way He designed women! I believe God is glorified when girls and women thank God for making them beautiful.

Pride is a vice all people have to watch out for, but quenching a woman's desire and opportunity to be beautiful is not going to make them humble—it will just drive them to find their sense of beauty in other flawed ways. They will live fighting their innate desire to be beautiful, because they are told it is sinful to enjoy being beautiful. Nothing could be farther from the truth. Believing that lie will create a sense of inferiority within the hearts of women who believe it, and at times it creates envy for those who are allowed to be beautiful.

I would be accurate to say that not many days go by in Ruthie's life that she does not hear me tell her she is beautiful. **This has never made Ruthie proud—and it never will.** I don't gauge my definition of beauty from this world—I define it the way God has taught me to define beauty. Even when Ruthie was pregnant and her belly was bigger than the planet Jupiter—even then, Ruthie was beautiful to me, and she knew it. I had seven daughters about whom I often remarked how beautiful they were, from young on up. But sadly, way back when my girls were growing up, I didn't know how vital it was for me as a father to affirm the beauty of my daughters so that they would develop a healthy identity. So looking back, I would have said it much, much more. Now that they are grown and married, I still tell them how beautiful they are.

Cloning

Cloning also denies a woman's voice in the group that values it. *Cloning* is requiring everyone to be the same—*likeness* instead of *individuality*. Cloning mandates women to deny their uniqueness and diversity and dress the same, or almost the same, as every other woman in their group. The way a person dresses reflects many things about the person, especially his or her personality. Ruthie values more formal clothing, and I value casual clothing and even sometimes a bit sloppy. But the way I dress represents who I am, not who someone else wants me to be.

Glorious Hair

1 Corinthians 11:15 says, *"But if a woman has long hair, it is a glory to her."* This verse tells me that God wants women to feel beautiful, and her hair is a large part of that identity.

Ruthie spends lots of time each day on her hair. So do most women. Most men wouldn't ever put the time into fixing their hair that women do. There is something about a woman's hair that is part of her female identity, and to hide it quenches something God gave to women as a gift. I couldn't care less about my hair. Thank God I have a wife who helps me be presentable in public for my own good.

A Primary False Motive behind Women Hiding Their Beauty

I'm not guessing about what I'm about to declare. In my decades of working with conservative people and ex-conservative people, I know this to be true. A primary motive behind hiding a women's beauty is so that men won't lust after them. Said another way, fear of sexual lust drives this practice.

I'm not against modesty. Modesty is a virtue, but you can drape a canvas tent over a woman, and it is not going to make men less lusty. Lust is a condition of the heart. But the ironic thing is that conservative religious communities are often the most lustful communities within Christendom. Pornography, immorality, incest, bestiality, and fornication are rampant in many, if not most, conservative cultures.

13

What's a Woman to Do?

A question Ruthie and I often get asked in the counseling room is, *what can I do if my influence is not valued?* You as a woman can't make other people hear your heart or respect your influence. But the first place you can start is the journey of undoing the lies you have believed about who you are. This journey will involve finding out through the Word of God what He believes about you. It will involve listening to the Holy Spirit in your heart revealing the places those lies exist. It will involve breaking your agreements with the false ways others have defined you in ways that God does not define you.

Many great books have been written on the glory of the woman as God created her. I won't list them now but ask God to show you what books to read as you search the Internet for Christian books for women .

Start using your voice more! In using your voice more you must put to death the spirit of people-pleasing and replace it with honor and obedience to God. Wherever you can, in the timing of God speak what you know, express what you feel, and share your heart with others.

Doing this won't make you brash, disrespectful, or abrasive. On the contrary, using your voice may enhance the beauty of your heart and help others to live better.

Stop feeling selfish when you *righteously* appeal for your own self-respect! People continually get selfishness and self-respect mixed up. Stop doubting or explaining away your emotional pain connected with not being celebrated for who you are. It is part of your inheritance in Christ Jesus!

Stop speaking through "hurt." In general, men can't talk to emotions. Speak through fact and truth when addressing a critical issue. If you were violated (a fact, according to you), say it and tell why. Mature people don't resolve problems through emotions, though emotions will be present, but they attempt to resolve problems objectively without subjective emotion. You may have to vent—I understand—but then shift to a healthier way of communicating.

Set boundaries! Submitting to a demeaning environment is not a healthy option, though I acknowledge that many women don't have a viable choice in the matter. I'll remind you of what I said in the beginning of this book regarding *two issues that are misaligned with the heart of God*:

1. Men who dominate women.
2. Women who surrender to it.

I'll address the marriage relationship here. For a marriage to thrive, it needs to be a win-win relationship. When a marriage digresses into a win-lose environment, it's in trouble. A win-lose marriage *is I get my way, you don't*. Both Ruthie and I had to get over feeling selfish when we tell what we need. Considering the insecurities Ruthie came into marriage with, I could easily have kept her in a "lose" mentality. She didn't know who she was, and she felt below me spiritually and intellectually. But I didn't want a *lose* wife, and I didn't want a *win-lose* marriage. It's not normal for your husband to get everything he wants and needs and for the wife to get crumbs, or for him to decide to do what he wants to do while your heart is laid painfully bare. Let me tell you one way Ruthie and I lived this out.

Barnes and Noble Nights

We lived in Iowa. The local bookstore at the mall, Barnes and Noble, had a coffee shop attached where Ruthie and I would often sit and chat. But on a regular basis Ruthie and I would go to the coffee shop with a planned agenda—*to strengthen our relationship.*

The store was always crowded—a prime location for the kind of discussion we were about to have. After some nice relational chatting, I would ask Ruthie, *how can I be a better husband and better meet your needs?* Ruthie would answer. There was nothing off limits. We would hold hands the whole time. Next Ruthie would ask me the same question, and I would answer.

When you're sitting in the middle of a crowded environment, you can't scream or yell or even show anger. That's why we did it there. And holding hands? Well, try holding hands when your spouse says something that makes you defensive—perhaps something you don't agree with. Immediately you want to pull back your hand, but at B&N, that was illegal. It kept us talking relationally, maturely, lovingly, and humble—brutally humble! At B&N we grew in our love for each other. We changed things. We made promises to each other. It got to the place where we looked forward to these times.

At the Barnes and Noble coffee shop both of us had an equal voice. One time, Ruthie's main complaint was how sloppily I dressed. She said, *"I'm tired of helping you to walk in the dignity God put upon you!"* She talked about two of my sweatshirts that were ragged, old, and sloppy. I disagreed and had a rebuttal. But we continued talking about it, and I realized that some of the scruffy ways I presented myself publicly were indeed embarrassing to her. I like her to look good, so why shouldn't she be allowed to like me looking good? I told her I would do my best to respect her wishes, inside knowing that what she felt was a good lesson for me to learn.

Beside the coffee shop was a Target store. I didn't tell her why we were going to Target. I bought two nice, new sweatshirts. I still wear my old ones when I'm bumming around, but I don't teach in them anymore. Ha!

I didn't just give in to Ruthie—I respected her and gave her a voice, realizing that my behavior and our oneness must be aligned. Of course, not all discussions end with me, or her, giving into a change. We take our challenges to God and decide how we can live together in the most honorable way. Some of the things we talked about in Barnes and Noble took quite some time to come to pass.

Are Men Bad Guys?

I will give you another perspective, one that does not water down anything I've written up to this point. First, I'll address you, the reader, as a wife, and then I'll address general leadership. But what I'm about to teach you applies to you both. Your husband may not be intentionally quenching your voice, your heart, your influence. He may be doing it because nobody ever told him he should or could call you to life. Perhaps he doesn't know how to, or his real desire is to call you to life, but he doesn't have permission because of the false theological mindset that you both are under. Could your own morbid view of yourself be a big part of the problem—but also could coming into a new God-view of yourself be a part of the solution? The best thing you can do for your husband is to break your agreements with **who you are not** and make your agreements with w**ho you are in Christ Jesus!**

What God thinks of any of us is always more glorious and good than we believe we are worthy of. But not to receive and believe what He says about you is a form of rebellion to the covenant of God. You are no less valuable than your husband. Your views and desires are no less important to your marriage and family. You have the potential to hear from God every bit as much as your husband. This is NOT coming OVER him but coming alongside him in the ONENESS God demands for a kingdom marriage. He must come alongside you also. Until you believe and receive your own transformed identity, you will never have the pleasure of being treated with value. I often say, *unless they are Holy-Spirit-filled people of love,* **nobody will ever treat you with more value than you treat yourself!** And as my friend and mentor Dale Mast says, *your greatest struggle in life is what you believe about YOU!* Your husband's good heart may be thrilled to have a wife who displays courage, confidence, and healthy self-respect and who is unwilling to listen to the accusations of the "accuser of our brethren" (Revelation 12:10, KJV).

But What If I Trust My Husband and am Happy to Have Him Make Some Decisions without My Input?

Problem: If your desire to let your husband lead in most situations without your voice is because you've become accustomed to being devalued, or if doing so is your hiding place to be safe, or if you don't think you have anything to offer—this is a problem!

Not a Problem: If your desire to let your husband lead in some situations without your voice is because you trust him as a good decision-maker, and you realize you are happy with your design as a follower, and your God-identity is intact—no problem. This is how Ruthie feels to a large degree. Sometimes she encourages me to lead by saying *I give her too much voice.* For us, this works well with Ruthie applying herself to her own callings and not having to feel responsible to make decisions she trusts me to make.

Taking a Risk at a Conservative Church

I was speaking two weeks in a row at a conservative church of around two hundred fifty people hungry for the things of the kingdom of God. Most had grown up in an Amish style of church. I was asked to speak on my book *Kingdom Culture* specifically about how to understand a *culture of honor*. The people were open, hungry for truth. There was a great spirit in the church.

I won't tell you all the details, but I want to tell you about something I did that was risky—again, I sensed that God was leading me to do it...

and it worked.

I asked the women in the congregation to respond to the question, *If you were in an important meeting of people, men and women, who needed to decide about something and you felt strongly about what decision should be made—but what you felt was different from what some of the men felt—what would keep you from sharing your thoughts?*

I thought I would have to pry the answers out of the women, but to my surprise the opposite happened—they were quick to vent their reasons (and I do mean vent!). One by one they shared amazing reasons that they would stuff their feelings in such a meeting. Here is a sampling of the reasons given:

- I would be afraid someone would think I was saying that my opinion was better than theirs.
- I would fear someone would judge me as being proud.
- I am a woman. My opinions are not as good as a man's. (This was said with obvious pain.)
- I would doubt that my thoughts were valid.
- I wouldn't want people to laugh at my comments.
- Women speaking in the presence of men is disrespectful, especially when they might disagree.

After the women were finished sharing, I taught them about their God-identity, fear of man, and how self-protection and the fear of man keeps them from being the voice of God to others. I told them that this grieves God!

Next I asked any woman who wanted to spiritually break off these demonic fears and insecurities and become who God designed them as women to be, to come forward. Many, if not most, of the women came forward, ready to break free from feeling under men and others. I prayed over them and declared freedom over them. I had them break their agreements with the lies that were holding them back.

My final step was a bigger risk. I then charged the leaders of the church to come to the front and pray over these women, release them, and call them to life. The leaders heartily responded.

It was an epic time to see woman emerging into a new season of identity as their church leaders called the women to life and affirmed their gifts from God.

Many of these leaders were not opposed to women being powerful—they just didn't know what to do with it. And when you don't know what to do with a woman who walks lovingly in self-respect and uses her voice—you stuff her into a box!

On a Lighter Note

I want to add this paragraph to lighten things up a bit so this book doesn't get too *heavy*. I want it to be *helpful*, not *heavy*. I decided to add it last night when Ruthie and I were driving through Lancaster, Pennsylvania, on *First Friday*. In the evening of the first Friday of each month, people flock to the core business section of Lancaster to hear music, eat outside, see art displays, meet friends, and generally have fun.

We were driving through the city and Ruthie said to me, "Bruce, of all these couples walking the streets, I think in about 99 percent of them the woman is talking." We laughed. Ruthie is like most women who like to talk. When Ruthie comes home from a meeting and tells me about it, she can condense a two-hour meeting into three hours. I can condense a two-hour meeting in three words, *it went fine*.

Studies say that women speak 20-25 thousand words a day, while men speak 7-10 thousand. For Ruthie and me, of course, it is not like her 20 thousand words to my 7 thousand; it's more like her 19,500 words to my 7,500. So though sometimes a woman doesn't use her *voice*, it does not mean she doesn't talk. A woman talks—and talks and talks! That's good, ladies. That's good! I mean don't *over-talk*, but talk!

Now back to the serious stuff!

14

Forbidden Leadership

Stacy and Jerel are some of our special friends whom Ruthie and I mentor and hang out with. They are about 35 years younger than us. We meet at the *Pancake House* regularly to chat, inspire each other, and enjoy Holy Spirit fellowship.

Recently I mentioned the process of God speaking to me about writing a book on releasing women to use their voices (the book you are now reading, which was not finished at the time). Both Stacy and Jerel had grown up in a conservative Mennonite culture.

I posed the question, *"In the Mennonite and Amish culture there are so many fantastic elements of family, holiness, and the fear of God, but why are there so many men in that culture who devalue women and fail to give equal value to a woman's voice?"*

Immediately Jerel responded, "Bruce, it's because they're afraid of women in leadership and think that when women express themselves, they're violating God and men by assuming leadership. This feels like sin to them!"

I had never thought about it that way. I said, "Women can be fantastic leaders. Why would they not want the leadership gift of a woman?"

I came home and looked up the word *usurp* in 1 Timothy 2:12 (KJV) in my Greek lexicon, where a woman is warned against u*surping authority over the man*. The word in the original Greek means *one who* *kills another*, one who acts on his own authority, *an absolute master*.

This phrase is not referring to faithful, loving, holy *ezers* who are walking in co- value with their husbands.

Happy Marriage or Kingdom Marriage

Ruthie and I were at Zig's Bakery & Café. I told her I was a visionary but would never succeed the way God wants me to succeed without her God-given spiritual giftings in my forward motion. That morning she had read the first portion of this book. I asked her for her opinions on it. She said to me, "Do you know what you're doing?"

I answered, "I'm not sure."

"Today you read me the draft of your new book, *Voice!* And today you're giving me my voice in asking me to review it, making sure it represents my heart too!"

The past month I united three couples in holy matrimony in just four weeks. That's not my usual schedule! In each of my challenges to the couples, I reminded them of what we had learned in our premarital counseling—the difference between a *happy marriage* and *a kingdom marriage*. Happy marriages are a dime a dozen, but kingdom marriages are rare. Kingdom marriages are those that follow the principles of holiness and remember that there is no fear in love, as recorded in 1 John 4:18. The culture of a kingdom marriage is not *what makes them happy* but *what God wants from their union*. Ruthie is my best friend, she is my lover, she is the one who walks beside me as an *ezer*. We would never have known how to have a marriage as fulfilling as it is without the guidance, direction, and voice of the Lord. I believe we have a kingdom marriage, which includes having a happy, fulfilled relationship. We walk in a way that both of us are equally valued.

15

Two More Items of Concern

I will mention the following two relevant issues because I feel it is important to do so, though this book is not the place to elaborate on them.

Narcissism

We might all benefit from being familiar with the term *narcissism*. Synonyms for *narcissism* include vanity, self-love, self-admiration, self-absorption, self-obsession, conceit, self-centeredness, egotism, egomania. There are various levels of narcissism, but the overriding focus is that narcissists are at the center of their own worlds. Some more that others, but narcissism always abuses others physically, emotionally, or spiritually.

In the region where I live, among a plethora of rules-based religions, hidden narcissism in marriages is rampant, embellished with Bible verses that support the abuse of women.

Narcissists know how to play people. They know how to look good. Often they know how to act humble and repentant, if in doing so they get affirmation. They are experts at making those who oppose them feel as if they are the ones who are wrong. But ultimately a narcissist does whatever he or she wants by crossing the boundaries of respect for others—denying them the freedom the narcissist himself or herself enjoys.

Not all men who devalue women are narcissists, but many of them are. And for those who *are* narcissists, many of them are **systemic narcissists**—self-centered abusers of women because of trauma, abuse, or parental wounding. But others are narcissists because they were taught that it's okay as a man to treat yourself to the delicacies you desire while denying women (specifically your wife) the privilege of having an equally abundant life. Lundy Bancroft in his book *Why Does He Do That? Inside the Minds of Angry and Controlling Men* tells women that one of the best ways to tell how deep a man's control problem goes is by seeing how he reacts when they start demanding that he treat them better. For some, control is macho maleness, for others it's flawed theology, and for others it is simply weak character. Many men act strong because inside they feel weak—a common characteristic of narcissists.

I am not shocked by non-Christians whose marriages reek of narcissism. Unholiness is the way of the world! But I continue to be dismayed by people who claim Christ who create cultures of narcissism in their marriage relationships and leadership paradigms. More and more I am aware of couples tolerating a narcissistic marriage relationship and deeming it as normal, or tolerating a narcissistic leader, pastor, or director under the guise of respecting authority. Among this group are wives waiting for the crumbs that drop from the master's table.

I am fully aware that women can be narcissistic, even though I perceive it far more in men.

Connection to Immorality

Though I don't enjoy telling you what I'm about to tell you, unfortunately it is something you must be aware of. As a sexual therapist for decades, I have discovered a pattern: **Men who demean women are far more apt to be immoral.** Also, many if not most, religious cultures that treat women as the lesser species are plagued with incest, pornography, and adultery. Often when Ruthie and I are counseling or mentoring a female from a religious culture, we expect more so than not that the girl has been sexually abused. This is sad. I have many stories I could tell to support the fact that religious cultures that devalue women are fertile grounds for immorality, but it is not for now in this book. Trust me—it's accurate.

Why is this? My view is that healthy sex must be connected to healthy intimacy. Healthy sex is "lovemaking." When a woman is not called to life by her husband and is living a "false self," she is not able to give full intimacy to the sexual arena of marriage, nor can the man. Without the power of God-ordained intimacy in marriage, based on true love, the only other option is lust.

Even outside of conservative religious cultures, you would find that narcissists are prone to lust and immorality. Extreme narcissists are almost always immoral.

In Closing

In closing I would like to admonish all the women reading this book: the men surrounding you—managers at work, your husband, spiritual authorities—may not give you the value you have been endowed with, and you may not have any other choice but to comply to their abuse. But even when you are devalued, you must still hold tightly deep in your heart the truth of who you are and whose you are—you are an equal child of the Creator God.

Two Additional Resources

Master vs. Father

A transition that every believer must make to relate to God the way He desires is to move from a master view of God to a Father mindset. In Islam, the Koran portrays Allah as a master. Jehovah, however, is an *ezer*—a servant-hearted God—Father to his people. If you view God or manage your pursuit of God in the master mindset, you will also lead others, and treat others, the way you believe about God. You will husband as a master, you will parent as a master, you will pastor as a master. I don't desire to take the space to embellish this thought, but if you are interested, one of the most impactful teachings that I have taught in years is recorded on my website, brucelengeman.com, called *Master vs. Father*. It deals with much more than what is in this short book.

My Follow-up Book

The book you are reading is somewhat of a follow-up book to one I wrote two years ago, *Come Alive to Her Heart: A Challenge to Married Men on Emotional Connecting*. It is available on Amazon. You can see it on my website, brucelengeman.com. I wrote this book to men who want to understand how to connect emotionally to their wives. Without destroying the maleness of manhood, I challenge men to lead the way to the oneness God desires in marriage. Check it out!

Okay, Bruce—when are you going to write a book addressing the flip side, how women can quench and devalue men? I'm not—Ruthie is. By the time you're reading this, her book may be available, but at the time I'm writing this , it's not finished. So...*stay tuned for Ruthie's book,* **Wind to His Back!**

Keep in Touch!

I would love to hear from you. Please email me brief (brief: short, concise), positive comments on what the Lord did in your heart because of reading *Voice!* (not a platform for arguments.) I will share these comments with others for their encouragement but will not put a name with them without asking your permission.

Email your comments to bruce.voicebook@gmail.com.

Other Teachings

While you're at it, check out my website at brucelengeman.com and sign up there for my newsletter, in which Ruthie and I share relevant resources, teachings, and videos. There you'll find links to all my other books. Also, look at my YouTube channel. Search for Bruce Lengeman, and then click on my picture. Click on the playlists for other relevant teachings.